You're Going to Talk to an AI Your Whole Life!

Learn to Understand It, Talk to It, and Use It Wisely —— Starting in School!

Gex Tekkino

Table of Contents

Module 1 – Understanding Artificial Intelligence
The basics of what AI is, how it works, and what it's used for.
Module 2 – Learning to communicate with an AI (prompting)
The art of asking the right questions to obtain useful, clear and precise answers.
Module 3 – Data and Privacy
What AI knows about you, how it uses data, and how to protect you.
Module 4 – Ethical, social and environmental issues
AI is not neutral: it raises questions of justice, equality, climate...
Module 5 – Using AI in Everyday Life
Create, correct, revise, code, organize:
practical cases to take action.
Module 6 – AI in schools and learning
AI can help you learn:
how to use it without becoming addicted.
Module 7 – AI in today's world
Transportation, health, justice, business, entertainment... AI is already everywhere.
Module 8 – AI in the world of tomorrow
Superintelligences, democracy, planet, future... And you, what role do you want to play?
Module 9 – Becoming a responsible digital citizen
Fake news, deepfakes, freedom of expression, autonomy in the face of AI.
Module 10 – GenAI and Intelligent Agents
Creative AI and AI assistants of the future: create, organize, act, with or without you.

And BONUS modules!
RAG, MCP, Agent2Agent, AGI, ASI

This book is for you

You hear about AI everywhere. On TV, on social media, in debates... But no one has really explained to you what it is, how it works, and especially what its use is in your life as a student.

This book is here for that. Not to scare you. Not to stuff your head with words. But to give you the power to understand, to take ownership, and to decide.

👀 **What does AI do for you?** To revise more intelligently, to create what you have in mind (texts, images, music, ideas, etc.), to save time... without cheating, to develop your critical thinking... And above all: to avoid being manipulated by machines that you don't understand.

🧠 **You were born in Generation AI.**
But AI shouldn't think for you.
It should help you think better.

So start this book. And prepare to understand, test, create, debate, and decide. This book is your training ground for the world of tomorrow.

And this world begins...now!

Module #01
Understanding AI

What is artificial intelligence?

How does an AI "learn"?

Weak AI vs. Strong AI

The AIs around you

The History of Artificial Intelligence

AI vs. Human: Differences and Complementarities

The major families of AI

and ❓ Questions to think about...

What is artificial intelligence?

Imagine a brain... that isn't human, but capable of learning, recognizing images, writing texts, proposing ideas, or even playing soccer with robots. This brain is what we call artificial intelligence—or AI, for short.

But be careful, AI doesn't think like you. It doesn't feel anything, it doesn't dream, it doesn't make jokes (unless it's been trained to do so). It analyzes data, spots patterns, and makes automatic decisions using very powerful programs.
For example :

- When you watch a video on YouTube, AI guesses what you'll like next.
- When you speak to a voice assistant like Siri or Alexa, the AI understands your request and responds.
- When you correct a text with ChatGPT, it is an AI that offers an improved version.

There are several types of AI, but the majority of AIs used today are called "weak": they are very strong in a specific area (playing chess, translating languages, recommending a series), but incapable of thinking like a human or doing several things at once.

In the fall, you'll learn how AI works, how to communicate with it, and, above all, how to maintain your critical thinking skills when faced with what it tells you. You'll see: it's not magic... but it is fascinating.

How does an AI learn?

Artificial intelligence isn't born intelligent. It learns, much like you do... but in a very different way!

Let's take an example: if you want to learn to recognize a cat, you look at several images, you observe the pointy ears, the whiskers, the body shape... Then, when you see a new animal, you can say: "It's a cat!" or "No, it's a dog." An AI does exactly that, but at high speed and with thousands of images. It is trained with examples. The more it sees, the more accurate it becomes. This process is called machine learning.

How does it work in practice?
1. We give the AI lots of data (examples).
2. She analyzes the common points.
3. She creates a model that allows her to make predictions (e.g., recognize a cat in a new image).

But be careful: if the examples are false or incomplete, the AI can learn the wrong things. This is why data quality is essential.

Another important point: an AI doesn't really understand what it sees. It spots patterns, it guesses, but it doesn't understand like you do. For example, an AI might mistake a black cat for an ink stain... if it's never seen a black cat during its training!

Weak AI vs. Strong AI

Not all artificial intelligence is equal. There are two broad categories: weak AI and strong AI.

🧠 Weak AI is what we use every day:
- It is designed to do one specific task.
- For example: recognizing faces, recommending videos to you, correcting text.
- She has no conscience, no general intelligence. She cannot reason like you.

These AIs are very effective, but very limited. ChatGPT, for example, is very good at answering questions, but it doesn't really understand what you're saying. It doesn't think; it predicts what you want to read.

🌐 Strong AI, on the other hand, is still a futuristic concept:
- She would have general intelligence, like a human.
- She could reason, adapt, learn on her own in any area.
- She would even be able to feel, perhaps to have a conscience.

But for now, no strong AI truly exists. It's still in science fiction movies or the dreams of some researchers. And many are wondering: is it really necessary to create such a powerful AI? What would the risks be?

The AIs around you

You may not realize it, but artificial intelligence is already everywhere in your daily life. It's hidden in the apps you use, the connected devices in your home, and even in the decisions some companies make about you.

Here are some concrete examples:

📱 On your phone
- – When you take a photo, the AI automatically improves the brightness.
- – When you type a message, the AI corrects mistakes or suggests the next word.

🎵 On your favorite apps
- – YouTube, Spotify, Netflix or TikTok use AI to recommend what you will like.
- – These AIs analyze your behavior: what you listen to, watch, like, or zap.

🚦 In the city
- – GPS predicts traffic using AI.
- – Self-driving cars (like Tesla's) use AI to "see" the road.

🏥 In health and research
- – AIs help detect certain diseases faster than doctors.

AI doesn't look like a giant robot with red eyes. It's silent, fast, and often invisible... but it's very influential. And the more you understand it, the more you can control it rather than be dependent on it.

The History of Artificial Intelligence

Artificial intelligence may seem very new, especially since the arrival of ChatGPT. However, the idea of a "thinking machine" goes back over 70 years! Here's a quick trip down memory lane:

1950 – Alan Turing The British mathematician poses a question that would become famous: "Can a machine think?" He devised a test (the Turing Test) to determine whether an AI could fool a human by talking to them.

1956 – Official birth of AI At a conference in Dartmouth (USA), researchers use the term "artificial intelligence" for the first time. This is the beginning of research!

1980s-2000s – Slow but Steady Progress Computers progressed, but AI remained limited to specific tasks (playing chess, recognizing characters). This was referred to as the "AI winter" because the results were disappointing at the time.

2010 – The big takeoff Thanks to big data (billions of data) and the power of processors, AI explodes:

– Siri (2011), Google Now (2012), Alexa (2014)...

– Facebook recognizes faces

– Google Translate is improving at high speed Since 2022 – Generative AI: With ChatGPT, DALL·E, Midjourney, AI can now write, summarize, invent, create images or music. It's a revolution visible to everyone... and you're right in the middle of it. But this is only the beginning.

You too are part of this story.

AI vs Human: differences and complementarities

Artificial intelligence is powerful, but it's not human. And that's a good thing!

Here are some key differences:
🧠 Human intelligence
– It is global and flexible: you can learn a language, play football, write a poem... all with one brain.
– You are able to feel emotions, have intuition, change your mind, improvise.
– You can ask yourself deep questions, invent completely new ideas, and understand the world meaningfully.
🤖 Artificial intelligence
– She is fast, specialized and tireless: she can read 1,000 texts in a minute, but only in one area at a time.
– She has no emotions or conscience. She doesn't understand what she's doing: she's following instructions.
– She is dependent on her training data: if she has never seen a pink elephant, she will not know what it is (even if you can imagine it).
But be careful: AI should not be seen as an enemy.
It can complement your abilities:

- It helps you go faster (summarize, correct, organize).
- It gives you ideas, which you can improve with your creativity.
- It automates boring tasks, leaving you time for the important things.

The secret is the AI + human alliance: a fast and powerful AI, driven by a smart mind. Yours!

The major families of artificial intelligence

Not all AI works the same way. In fact, they can be divided into three broad families, based on how they make decisions and learn.

🧠 1. Symbolic (or "logical") AI

This is the oldest. It works with precise rules written by humans. For example: "IF temperature > 37.5°C, THEN fever alert." It doesn't learn by itself, but it is reliable for well-defined tasks.

👉 Use: calculator, medical expert system, diagnostic assistant.

🔄 2. AI by learning (or machine learning)

It learns from data, without being given all the rules. It analyzes examples and deduces patterns (like recognizing a dog in an image). It is the most widely used method in modern applications today.

👉 Uses: facial recognition, machine translation, YouTube recommendations.

🎨 3. Generative AI This is the new star of AI!

It is capable of creating content: text, images, sound, video, code... It is based on very powerful models like deep neural networks (deep learning).

👉 Use: ChatGPT, DALL·E, Midjourney, music or game generators. Each family of AI has its strengths and limitations. Understanding them will help you better understand how to use it... and when to be wary.

? Questions to reflect on

What is artificial intelligence?

- Can you think of three times in your day when you used AI without realizing it?
- What differentiates an artificial intelligence from a human?
- Can an AI have emotions or opinions? Why?
- Do you think an AI should be able to make important decisions for you? In what cases?
- Does AI impress you, worry you, or amuse you? Why?

How does an AI learn?

- If you had to teach an AI what pizza is, what would you show it?
- Why do you need to give an AI lots of examples?
- Do you think AI can learn from mistakes? How?
- Is it dangerous if AI is trained with bad data? Why?
- In your opinion, what can an AI do better than a human? And what can it do worse?

Weak AI vs. Strong AI

- What AI do you use most often today? Is it a weak AI?
- In your opinion, what would make an AI "strong"?
- Should a strong AI have rights, like a human?
- Do you think we will ever be able to create an AI as intelligent as a human brain?
- Do you find it reassuring or worrying to know that no strong AI exists yet?

The AIs around you
-
- Which app on your phone do you think uses AI?
- Have you ever been surprised by an AI recommendation?
- Do some AIs really make your life easier? Which ones?
- How do you feel about AI observing you or analyzing your behavior?
- Would you like some daily tasks to be done by an AI?

The History of Artificial Intelligence
- What date stands out to you most in this AI story? Why?
- Do you think the Turing Test is still valid today?
- Do you feel that AI is evolving too fast, not fast enough, or just in time?
- What AI-related event has impressed you the most in recent years?
- What do you think AI will look like in 10 or 20 years?

AI vs. Human: Differences and Complementarities
- In what areas are you clearly better than an AI?
- What does an AI do better than you today?
- Do you think we should be afraid of AI's capabilities?
- How could you use it to improve your daily life?
- In your opinion, should we put limits on the uses of AI?

The major families of artificial intelligence
- Which of these three AI families do you think is most useful? Why?
- Did you know that an AI could create images or music?
- Do you think it is necessary to say when an image or text is generated by AI?
- Do you prefer a logical, learning, or creative AI?
- In what area would you like to see an AI help you or create something for you?

Module #02
Learn Prompting

What is a prompt?

Effective Prompts: Golden Rules

Examples of good prompts

Create your own prompt

Prompt in different contexts

and ? Questions to think about...

What is a prompt?

A prompt is an instruction that you give to an artificial intelligence so that it responds to you.

It's the way you talk to him, as if you were giving a mission to a super fast assistant.
🗣 Basically, when you write in ChatGPT:
"Tell me a joke about unicorns."
...you just made a prompt!

A good prompt allows the AI to understand exactly what you want. But if your question is vague or too vague, the answer may be off the mark.
Example:
- ✕ "Say something funny."   Too vague.
- ✅ "Make up a short joke about a unicorn playing soccer." More specific, funnier!

🔧 Some useful prompt types:
- Create: "Write a sad poem about a robot lost in space."
- Learn: "Explain photosynthesis to me as if I were 10 years old."
- Organize: "Make me a revision schedule for the brevet."
- Imagine: "Invent a video game character that is half-human and half-dog."

In the following pages, you will see how to improve your prompts to become a master of dialogue with AI!

Effective prompts: the golden rules

Asking an AI a question is like giving a mission to a super-fast assistant. But for that mission to succeed, your message must be clear, precise, and well-structured.

Here are the 4 golden rules for writing an effective prompt:

🥇 1. Be clear and precise Avoid vague sentences like "Tell me about an animal." Prefer: "Describe an imaginary animal that lives in the sea and can fly."

🥈 2. Give context Tell the AI who it is talking to or why you are asking the question.
Example: "Explain climate change to a 4th grader."

🥉 3. Set a goal What do you really want to achieve? A text? A list? An original idea? "Give me 3 ideas for funny stories to write in class."

🎯 4. Assign a role to the AI Ask it to "play" a character to improve the quality of the answers. "You are a history teacher. Summarize the French Revolution in 10 lines."

🛠️ Bonus tip:
You can always refine your prompt after the response, just like in a real conversation. The more you talk, the better your response will get.

Good prompts vs. bad prompts

You now know that the quality of an AI's response depends directly on your question. Here are some concrete examples to help you understand what to do... and avoid:

🎨 Create a story ✕ Write a story.

   Too vague. The AI doesn't know what genre, length, or for whom.

✅ Write a short, funny story for a 4th grader about a hamster who becomes president.

   Precise, clear, and fun. AI knows what to do.

📚 Review a lesson ✕ Explain the French Revolution to me.

   Too broad. You risk an incomprehensible text.

✅ You are my history teacher. Summarize the major causes of the French Revolution in 5 simple points.

   Targeted, useful, well-structured.

🗿 Ask a complex question ✕ Give me ideas for a presentation.

   AI does not know the subject, nor the class, nor the duration.

✅ Give me 3 ideas for original SVT presentations for a 5-minute presentation in 4th grade.

   Context + objective = relevant result.

🛠️ You can always have fun turning an average prompt into a great one. It's a real skill, a bit like learning how to ask good questions in class.

Create your own prompt

Now that you know what a prompt is, how it works, and how to improve it, it's time to get started!
Here's a short guided workshop to help you create your own prompt, test it, and then improve it.

🎯 Step 1 – Choose your goal

Ask yourself what you really want the AI to do:
☑️ Tell a story?
☑️ Explain a lesson to you?
☑️ Help you organize something?
☑️ Help you create an image, music, code?

🧱 Step 2 – Build your prompt Use the 4 golden rules:

- Be clear and precise
- Gives context
- Set a goal
- Assign a role to AI

⚙️ Step 3 – Test and correct

☑️ Type your prompt into an AI (like ChatGPT or another) 👀 Read the response 🔁 Ask yourself: is it satisfactory? Is something missing? 🧠 If necessary, modify your prompt to make it even more effective.

💡 Inspiring example:
🎯 Objective: Learn the history of electricity ✏️ Prompt: You are a passionate science teacher. Explain to me how electricity was discovered, in 5 easy-to-remember steps, as if I were a middle school student.

Prompt in different contexts

Now you know how to create a good prompt. But did you know that you can use this skill in almost every area of your life? Here are some examples to inspire you:

🎒 At school
- *"Explain the Pythagorean theorem to me as if I were in 8th grade."*
- *"Summary Chapter 2 of the novel 'The Wave' in 5 points."*
- *"Make me a revision sheet on volcanoes, Year 10 level."*

AI can help you understand, summarize, and organize your ideas.

🧠 To learn differently
- *"Take a 10-question quiz on the French Revolution with answers."*
- *"Teach me 5 German words with a simple dialogue."*

AI becomes your revision coach or your personal language teacher.

🎨 To create
- *"Invent a fun puzzle for an escape game in a college."*
- *"Write a sad song about a panda moving."*
- *"Make an acrostic poem with the word INTELLIGENCE."*

You can have fun creating, imagining, inventing.

🧍 To organize and think
- *"Give me a 2-week revision schedule with breaks."*
- *"Help me manage my stress before a test."*
- *"Note 3 good habits to sleep better during exams."*

AI can be a caring personal assistant.

❓ Questions to reflect on

What is a prompt?

- Have you ever used a prompt without knowing what it was called?
- Why do you think a specific prompt gives better answers?
- In what areas do you think a well-formulated prompt can really help you?
- Are you more creative, practical, or curious when you ask an AI a question?
- If you had to teach someone how to make a good prompt, what would you tell them first?

Effective Prompts: The Golden Rules

- Which rule helps you most understand how to better formulate a prompt?
- Have you ever gotten a strange or disappointing answer? Why?
- Could you use these rules for your homework? Which ones?
- In your opinion, should we always guide AI... or give it freedom?
- Can you write a prompt following the 4 golden rules? Try it!

Good prompts vs. bad prompts

- Have you ever gotten a wrong answer because of a vague prompt?
- Which of these good prompts made you want to try it with an AI?
- Have you ever made a good prompt without knowing it?
- Why does giving AI a role often improve the quality of the response?
- Can you rewrite a prompt you've already used to make it better?

Create your own prompt

- What is your personal goal for this prompt?
- Are you satisfied with the AI's response? Why?
- What did you change to improve it?
- Do you feel more comfortable talking to an AI now?
- What prompt idea would you like to try next?

Prompt in different contexts

- What example made you want to try a new prompt?
- What homework or project could AI help you with this week?
- Have you ever used AI to create something fun?
- Do you think AI should be used in all subjects?
- In what context would you not use AI? Why?

Module #03
Data & Privacy

Personal data: what is it?

AI needs data...

Privacy and GDPR

Protecting your information: simple reflexes

Can you delete your data?

and ❓ Questions to think about...

Personal data: what is this ?

When you browse the internet, like a video, or fill out a form, you leave digital traces. This information is called personal data.
But what exactly is personal data?

This is any information that allows you to be identified directly or indirectly.

📌 Examples of personal data:
- Your name, first name, address, email
- Your age, date of birth, gender
- Your profile picture
- Your Internet searches
- Your location (geolocation)
- Your habits (movies watched, music listened to, games played)

This data is often collected automatically, recorded, and then analyzed by companies... or artificial intelligence.
Why? To offer you personalized content, target ads, or improve a service.

⬤ The problem is that sometimes:
- You don't know you're giving this information away.
- You don't control how they are used.
- You can even be profiled without realizing it!

This is why it is essential to know your rights and to think before you click.

AI needs data... so what?

AI isn't magic: it doesn't guess anything. To function, it needs to learn from thousands, even billions of data points.

It's simple:

⬇ No data   No AI.

📊 Lots of data   Powerful AI.

📚 How does it work?

Let's take ChatGPT as an example:

– He was trained with huge amounts of text: books, articles, websites...

– He identified language patterns (how words are linked together, how we answer a question).

– Then it can generate text, but from what it has seen.

The same goes for facial recognition AI: it saw millions of faces to "learn" to recognize human features.

🔍 Why is this a sensitive subject?

The data used may be:

- Public (like Wikipedia),
- Private (like messages or searches),
- Or personal, sometimes recovered without your clear consent.

When an AI is poorly supervised, it can: – Reproduce biases (prejudices contained in the data),

– Use data without respect for privacy,

– Learning things that are false, incomplete or shocking.

This is why we must be vigilant about data sources... and what we share ourselves!

Privacy and GDPR

When you use a website, an app, or an AI tool, you often share personal data. But you're not defenseless! In France (and throughout Europe), there's a law to protect your privacy: the GDPR.

🛡 What is GDPR?
The General Data Protection Regulation, or GDPR, is a European law that came into force in 2018.
It requires companies, apps, websites, and AI to respect your personal data.

📋 Your rights thanks to the GDPR
1. The right to information means you need to know what data is collected, why, and by whom.
2. The right to consent, no data can be collected without your clear consent (e.g. cookies).
3. The right of access, you can request what data a company holds on you.
4. The right of rectification, you can correct an error in your personal information.
5. The right to be forgotten: you can request the deletion of your data, except for legal exceptions.
6.

And what about AI in all this?
AI tools must also comply with GDPR, even if they process billions of data points. But this isn't always easy to control.
This is why users (you!) must be vigilant:
Read the terms of use, Refuse non-essential cookies, Ask yourself: "Do I really want to share this?"

Protect your information: simple reflexes

Now that you know what personal data and the GDPR are, let's see how to protect yourself on a daily basis.

You don't need to be a hacker or an expert: a few good habits are enough to keep control of your digital life.

💡 Here are 6 simple reflexes to adopt:
Read (at least a little) what you agree to.
    Before you click "I accept the terms," take a look: some sites track you without you realizing it.
Use strong passwords.
    A password = 3 things mixed together: capital letters + numbers + symbols. Ex: Tiger42!Sun.
Enables two-factor authentication.
    An extra code to log in: a small gesture, but a big protection.
Don't share everything on social media.
    Address, school, number... no need for everyone to know everything.
Check app permissions.
    Does a game really need your location or microphone?
Do your digital cleaning regularly.
    Delete accounts or apps you no longer use. Less data = less risk.

🧠 The important thing is not to have zero trace, it's to be aware of what you share... and to choose to do so.

Can you delete your data?

You've probably heard: "The internet never forgets." But is that really true? Can you delete your data whenever you want?
✅ The answer: yes... but it's not that simple.

In theory, you have the right to request the deletion of your data, thanks to the famous "right to be forgotten".

You can :
- Delete an account (social network, app, service)
- Send a removal request to a site
- Ask a search engine (like Google) to stop showing a page that talks about you

But in practice...   It's not 100% guaranteed
– Some companies keep data in cache or on secondary servers.
– Others share your information with partners... without you knowing.
– If someone took a screenshot or reposted your content, it may continue to circulate even after deletion.

💡 So what to do?
– Think before you post or share.
– Be sparing with personal information.
– And don't hesitate to assert your rights: sites like CNIL.fr can help you send an official request.
On the internet, your digital footprint follows you. It's up to you to choose what you want to leave behind... and what you want to erase.

? Questions to reflect on

Personal data: what is it?

- Can you name a piece of personal information that you give out without thinking about it?
- Have you ever filled out a form without knowing why it was asking for certain information?
- Why do you think some apps want to know your location?
- Do you ever read the terms of use before signing up somewhere?
- What personal data do you consider most sensitive? Why?

AI needs data... so what?

- Why does AI need so much data?
- Do you think everything you find on the internet is reliable?
- Have you ever posted personal information without thinking about how you would use it?
- Would you be okay with an AI learning from your private messages?
- How could data collection be better regulated?

Privacy and GDPR

- Have you ever seen a GDPR banner on a website? Did you know what it was?
- Which of these rights do you think is most important? Why?
- Have you ever accepted cookies without reading what you were agreeing to?
- Do you think an AI should have the right to keep your data for life?
- What would you do if an AI used your data without your consent?

Protecting your information: simple reflexes

- How many different passwords do you use? Are they really secure?
- Do you enable two-factor authentication when it is offered?
- What was the last service or app you gave your number or address to?
- Have you ever regretted posting something on a social network?
- What rule could you apply today to better protect your information?

Can you delete your data?

- Have you ever deleted an account or content? Why?
- Do you think a search engine should really archive everything?
- If an AI keeps data about you without your consent, what would you do?
- Do you think students should be taught how to "clean up" their online presence?
- In your opinion, should everyone have the right to total digital oblivion?

Module #04
Ethical and social issues

AI biases

AI and employment

The ecological footprint of AI

Can we trust an AI?

AI and Education: Help or Risk?

Can AI create art?

and ? Questions to think about...

AI biases

Do you think an AI is always objective? That it gives the same answer to everyone? Well, no. Like humans, artificial intelligences can have... biases.

! What is bias?
Bias is a distortion or injustice in the way an AI processes information. This can include stereotypes, omissions, or errors that disadvantage certain people or groups.
But be careful: this isn't because AI is evil. It's because it learns from human data... which isn't always perfect.

Concrete examples of bias: A recruitment AI that selects mostly men because it was trained on men's CVs; facial recognition software that recognizes lighter faces better than darker ones because it has seen fewer examples of diversity - and a chatbot that makes racist or sexist comments... because it has read too much toxic content on the internet. Result: unfair, unequal, and even dangerous decisions if no one corrects them.

What to do about this?
– Monitor data used to train AI.
– Test AI in different contexts to identify injustices.
– Train developers in ethics, and teach you to keep a critical eye.

AI has no opinion... but it can inherit the worst aspects of humanity if we're not careful.

AI and employment

Artificial intelligence hasn't just changed our apps...it's also starting to transform the world of work.

Some professions evolve, others disappear, and new professions appear.

📉 Jobs under threat?
AI can automate repetitive or rule-based tasks. 🖐 Examples: Accounting, sorting files, proofreading legal documents, self-checkouts, voice commands in fast food restaurants, and automated journalism for sports scores or weather. These jobs won't necessarily disappear... but they will change. Humans will often have to collaborate with AI, or focus on more creative, human, or complex tasks.
📈 Jobs that are emerging (or exploding)

And AI also creates a whole host of new needs: AI Engineer, Model Trainer, AI Ethics Specialist, Prompt Designer (the one who knows how to ask AI the right questions), AI-Generated Content Detector, and Human-Machine Mediator.
Some current professions will simply integrate AI into their tools: teachers, doctors, designers, developers, communicators... 🕐 And for you?
Even if you don't want to become a computer scientist, knowing about AI gives you an advantage.
Because in the future, almost every job will have some AI component.   It's better to work with it... than to endure it!

The ecological footprint of AI

When you talk to an AI like ChatGPT, you're not lighting a factory, an engine, or a chimney. Yet, artificial intelligence consumes a lot of energy.

Why? Because before answering your question, she had to be trained... and that's very polluting.

⚙ Why does AI pollute?

1. Model training. An AI like ChatGPT has been "trained" with billions of texts. This requires months of calculations on supercomputers.　It's like running thousands of computers non-stop for weeks.
2. Servers are running continuously. Every time you talk to an AI, your request goes to a data center, often halfway around the world, and then comes back with a response.　These servers consume a lot of electricity and require very demanding cooling systems.
3. Billions of uses per day. The more popular AI becomes, the more it's used... the more it consumes. And the impact grows every second.

💡 For example: A simple question asked to an AI can consume as much electricity as a light bulb left on for several minutes - and - Training models would emit around 500 tons of CO_2: the equivalent of several dozen Paris-New York flights.

🌱 What can be done? – Optimize AI models to make them less power-hungry – Use green electricity in data centers – Limit unnecessary or repetitive uses

Can we trust an AI?

You ask ChatGPT a question, and it answers in a second. You ask DALL·E for an image, and it magically appears.
But... can you trust him completely?
Not always.

What AI can do very well:
✅ Summarize, rephrase, generate ideas ✅ Classify, translate, create original content ✅ Save you time... and even make you laugh!
But be careful: AI doesn't understand what it's saying. It doesn't always check the facts. It doesn't know if what it writes is true, false, dangerous, or absurd.
❇️ The limits of trust
1. She can make up information   This is what we call a "hallucination". She answers you confidently, but it's false.
2. It can be influenced by its data   If it has been trained on biased content, it can reproduce stereotypes or errors.
3. It has no personal opinion   AI has no conscience, no morals, no emotions. It responds according to what it has been taught... or what it has "seen".
4. She doesn't know what you really want   If your prompt is unclear, she may offer you an answer that's off the mark.
🔑 The real solution? You. Learning to use AI is like learning to use a search engine or a calculator: 📌 You have to verify, cross-check, analyze.

AI is a powerful tool, but you must be in control.

AI and education: help or risk?

You may already be using AI to help you with your homework, summarize a text, or correct a typo. Good idea? Bad idea?

As is often the case with AI... it depends on how you use it.

☑️ When AI can be a great ally AI can: Explain a concept to you differently, in a simpler or clearer way; Save you time with revision cards or quizzes; Help you reformulate a text or organize your ideas; and Motivate you to learn with fun formats (games, simulations, etc.) 💡 If you use it to learn and progress, it's a great tool.

When AI can become a problem But be careful... AI can also make you lazy if:
- You ask him to do all the work for you.
- You copy and paste an answer without understanding
- You cheat during an assignment or presentation

In this case, you're not developing your ideas, your understanding, or your confidence. And then, some teachers can easily recognize a text written by AI (too perfect, too vague, too repetitive, etc.).

🎯 The ideal? Learn with AI, not just through it. You can use it as a coach, an assistant, or a mirror... but you remain the pilot.
AI does not replace your reasoning, your creativity, your judgment.

Can AI create art?

A moving poem, an original painting, a catchy song... If an AI produced them, is it still art? Or just a well-programmed imitation?

🤖 What AI can do Generative AIs like DALL·E, ChatGPT or Suno can today:
- Write a poetic text or a song
- Create an image from a simple prompt
- Compose original music
- Generate videos, logos, voices...

They draw on millions of existing examples, learn styles, forms... and recombine all of that in a new way.

🎭 But is it really creation?

An AI feels nothing. It knows neither the artistic intention, nor the emotion, nor the suffering or joy that lie behind a work.
She doesn't create from a personal story, she creates from what she's seen. It's amazing... but is it that profound?
Some believe AI can be an inspirational tool for human artists, like a digital paintbrush. Others say it's not art because there's no soul behind it.

🖼️ And you, what do you think?
Can we be moved by a work generated by AI? Can we applaud a song that no human actually wrote?

The line between art, technology and illusion is becoming blurred...

? Questions to reflect on

AI biases

- Have you ever seen an algorithm or app give an unfair result?
- Why do you think AI "reproduces" our stereotypes?
- What should be done to make AI fairer?
- Should AI be mandatory testing to avoid bias?
- In your opinion, can a biased human create a completely fair AI?

AI and employment

- Do you know of a job that has changed because of AI?
- Are you afraid that a robot will do your future job for you?
- In your dream job, how could AI help you?
- Do you prefer a job with or without technology? Why?
- If you had to invent a new job related to AI, what would it be?

The ecological footprint of AI

1. Are you surprised to learn that AI consumes so much energy?
2. Should we limit the use of AI to protect the environment?
3. Have you ever used an AI just "to see" without a specific goal?
4. Do you think companies should be required to use clean energy to run their AI?
5. What can you do, at your level, to use AI more responsibly?

Can we trust an AI?

- Have you ever believed an AI answer… that turned out to be wrong?
- How do you verify what an AI tells you?
- Is a human always more reliable than an AI?
- Should the use of AI be banned in certain cases (medical, justice, politics, etc.)?
- In your opinion, should we always clearly state that content was generated by AI?

AI and Education: Help or Risk?

- Have you ever used AI to help you with an assignment? For what purpose?
- Have you learned anything from AI that you didn't understand before?
- Do you think it's cheating if AI helps you organize your ideas?
- What limits should be placed on the use of AI in schools?
- How could you use AI to progress without losing your autonomy?

Can AI create art?

- Have you ever seen or heard of an AI creation? Did it impress you?
- In your opinion, do you need to have emotions to create "real" art?
- Would you be comfortable with a movie, music or comic book made 100% by AI?
- Can AI be a source of inspiration for humans? Why?
- Should we require clear disclosure when a work is generated by AI?

Module #05
In action with AI

Your first test with ChatGPT

Create an image with AI

Correct a text with AI

Code a little (Python or Scratch)

Imagine an AI for your class / your daily life

and ❓ Questions to think about...

Your first test with ChatGPT

What if it was time to get started?

You understand what AI is, how it learns, how to talk to it, and what its challenges are...

Now it's time to test for yourself what ChatGPT can do.

🖊 Objective: to communicate with an AI You will ask a real prompt, get a response, then compare it to what you expected.

You'll see: sometimes, AI can surprise you, help you... or make you think about how to better formulate your request.

🔧 Step 1 – Prepare your prompt Choose a simple topic that interests you and write a clear prompt.

✏️ Examples:
- *You're my biology teacher. Explain to me the difference between an animal cell and a plant cell.*
- *Tell me a funny story about a ninja cat and a volcano.*
- *Help me revise my lesson on the First World War in 5 key points.*

💻 Step 2 – Use ChatGPT (or another AI of your choice)

Go to a generative AI site (like chat.openai.com, Mistral, or an authorized school tool)   Paste your prompt   Read the answer carefully

🧠 Step 3 – Analyze your answer

Ask yourself these questions:
- Is the answer clear?
- Is it what you expected?
- Are there any mistakes, or anything surprising?
- How could you improve your prompt to get an even better response?

🛠️ AI is like a mirror: it reflects the clarity of your thinking.

Create an image with AI

What if you could turn an idea in your head into a real image, in just a few seconds? That's exactly what AI solutions like DALL·E, MidJourney, and Stable Diffusion offer. They can generate images from simple sentences. This is what we call text-to-image.

🔍 How does it work?

You write a prompt (a textual instruction), and the AI interprets your words to create an original image.

Examples of prompts:

- *An astronaut cat playing guitar on the moon, cartoon style*
- *A futuristic city in the middle of the jungle, in digital painting*
- *An origami dragon flying over a Japanese castle, realistic style*

💡 The more precise your prompt is (style, atmosphere, colors, action), the more impressive the image will be.

🎨 Workshop – Create your image

1. Choose a visual AI
2. Write your creative prompt
3. Run the build and observe the result
4. If necessary, modify your prompt to refine the image

🧠 What is it for?

You can use these AIs to:

- Illustrate a story or presentation
- Create a logo, a poster, a comic book character
- Imagining worlds for a game or a novel
- Explore your creativity... even if you don't know how to draw!

Correct a text with AI

You have written a text for an assignment, a letter, a dialogue or a story... and you are wondering if it is clear, well written, without mistakes?
You can ask an AI to correct it — but be careful: it doesn't do the work for you, it helps you improve.

💼 What AI can fix:
✅ Spelling or grammar mistakes ✅ Sentences that are too long or confusing ✅ Repetition of certain words ✅ Style (more fluid, clearer, more suited to your level) 🔹 Example, your original text:
"I want to learn to write better because it's important for my future. People judge you when you make mistakes; it shows you're not serious."
🤖 AI Response:
"I want to learn to write better because it's important for my future. People judge you when you make mistakes: it shows a lack of seriousness."
👉 Do you see the difference? It's still your idea, your intention... but better formulated.
🛠️ Workshop – Correct your text with AI
  1. Write a short text of 3 to 5 lines (description, opinion, mini-story)
  2. Paste it into an AI like ChatGPT or Grammarly
  3. Observe the proposed corrections
  4. Analysis: What did you learn? What could you have corrected yourself?

📌 Remember: AI is a tool, not a magic corrector.
You remain the author, and you must always understand the corrections to truly progress.

Code a little (Python or Scratch)

You don't need to be a computer pro to start coding with AI!

You can learn how to create simple little instructions in Python (the basic language of AI) or Scratch (a visual language widely used in middle school).

The important thing is not to write 100 lines of code... but to understand how a machine "thinks".

🧱 What is code?
Code is a language for giving orders to a machine.

Examples of bases:
```
print("Hello!")
```
   The computer displays "Hello!" on the screen.

You can also create a function that acts based on what you give it:
```
def hello(name):
    print("Hello " + name + " !") hello("Max")
```
   The computer displays: Hi Max!

and with Scratch...

🐱 With Scratch, it's even simpler!

Scratch uses colored blocks to code without writing.
You can :
- Make a character (the cat) move
- React to clicks
- Ask questions
- Display a message

You can practice here: https://scratch.mit.edu

🤖 And with AI?
You can also ask an AI to help you code!
Example prompt for ChatGPT:
Write a small program in Python that asks for my first name and says hello.

AI gives you the code, which you can read, modify, and test.

The important thing is not just to have the result, but to understand what each line does.

Imagine an AI for your daily life

You've discovered how AI works, how to communicate with it, how to use it to learn, create, correct, code... But now, what if you were the one to invent an AI? An AI that's useful to you, in your everyday life.

🧠 Examples of "everyday" AI 🤖 An AI that helps you manage your stress before a test 🤖 An AI that invents meals for you with what's left in your fridge 🤖 An AI that teaches you a new language while playing 🤖 An AI that helps you revise and encourages you 🤖 An AI that composes music according to your mood The idea is not to create a science fiction robot, but a simple, useful, ethical, responsible intelligence. An AI that would make your life better, without replacing you.

💡 **Your creative challenge**
1. Give your AI a name (original, funny, stylish)
2. What is it for? What problem does it solve?
3. How does it interact with you? Voice? Text? App?
4. What emotion does she give off? Friendly? Serious? Zen? Energetic?
5. What ethical rules would she follow?

Creating an AI also means thinking about the impact it can have on you, on others, and on the world. And you, what AI would you dream of seeing exist tomorrow?

❓ Questions to reflect on

Your first test with ChatGPT

- What surprised you about your first AI response?
- Was it better or worse than what you could have done alone?
- What did you learn about asking a good question?
- Did you want to talk more with the AI?
- Do you think this experience can help you with your homework or projects?

Create an image with AI

- Did the generated image match what you had in mind?
- Did you feel more creative with the help of AI?
- Do you think an artist can be inspired by AI to create?
- Could you use this type of tool for a school project?
- In your opinion, has AI replaced the role of the designer in your image?

Correct a text with AI

- What did you think of the AI's proposed corrections?
- Did this help you better understand your mistakes?
- Did you want to write a more polished text from the start?
- Do you feel more confident writing now?
- In which subjects could you use this help without cheating?

Code a little (Python or Scratch)

- Have you ever tried coding something? With what tool?
- What difference do you see between Python and Scratch?
- Did it help you to see how AI writes code?
- In what project would you like to use some programming?
- Do you think all students should learn the basics of coding? Why?

Imagine an AI for your daily life

- Does your AI help you become more independent or more dependent?
- Does your AI respect your privacy?
- Who would have the right to use your AI?
- What would you do if your AI made a major mistake?
- Should your AI have limits? What are they?

Module #06
AI in schools and learning

How AI Personalizes Learning

Can AI replace a teacher?

Reviewing with AI: Effective Methods

Create a personalized revision plan

Learning to learn with AI

and **?** Questions to think about...

How AI Personalizes Learning

Imagine a teacher who knows you by heart:

He knows what you have understood... and what you have not yet retained.

He explains things to you in your own way, according to your pace, your style, your mistakes.

He encourages you when you're stuck, challenges you when you've mastered it.

Artificial intelligence is beginning to approach this ideal teacher.

An AI can analyze your progress More and more educational tools use AI to: Track your level in real time, Adapt exercises according to your difficulty, Identify your recurring errors - and offer you targeted revisions This is what we call adaptive learning. You progress at your own pace, without being slowed down or lost.

Concrete examples: Apps like Khan Academy, Kartable or SchoolMouv already offer personalized content; Some tools (like ChatGPT) can explain a lesson to you based on your level: "explain it to me as if I were in 8th grade"; AI can generate quizzes, mind maps, summaries... just for you.

A powerful tool... but to be used with balance AI does not replace the teacher. It cannot:

- Read your emotions
- Create a human connection
- Adapting a course to an entire class in interaction

It's a complementary tool that can boost your motivation, your autonomy, and your confidence.

Can AI replace a teacher?

You ask an AI a question. It answers quickly. You ask it for a summary, an exercise, an explanation... and it does it.
So, does this mean that one day teachers will be replaced by machines? Spoiler: not so fast!

🤖 What AI can do (very well)
- Give a clear, short explanation, adapted to your level
- Create a custom exercise or interactive quiz
- Summarize a text, correct an essay, translate a word
- Follow you 24/7 without getting tired

AI is fast, accurate, always available... but it works alone.

🧑 What a teacher does... that an AI will never be able to do
- Adapting to an entire class, with its moods and dynamics
- Motivate you, reassure you, congratulate you, refocus you
- Create an atmosphere, make people want to learn
- Understanding your deep blocks, not just grammatical mistakes
- Make you laugh, tell an anecdote, change methods at the right time

A teacher doesn't just teach a curriculum. They also teach you confidence, curiosity, respect, and listening.

💡 AI + the teacher = the ideal duo AI can free up the teacher's time by automating certain tasks. The teacher, on the other hand, can focus on real human relationships. Together, they can offer you a richer and more personalized learning experience.

Review with AI: effective methods

Do you have a test to prepare for? A lesson to remember? A presentation to organize?

Good news: AI can become your personal revision assistant, provided you know how to ask it the right things.

💼 What you can do with AI to revise
✅ Course summary "Summarize the main stages of the Second World War in 5 points." ✅ Vocabulary sheet "Give me a sheet of 10 important words to know about human reproduction." ✅ Targeted exercise "Give me a 4th grade math exercise on the Pythagorean theorem, with correction." ✅ Quick quiz "Ask me 5 multiple-choice questions on energy in physics and chemistry." ✅ Tailor-made explanation "Explain the concept of democracy to me as if I were in 4th grade, with an example."

🧠 The rules to make it really work: Prepare your prompt carefully; Test several formulations if the first answer doesn't suit you; Note down what you remember, reformulate in your own words Don't just read: interact! And (ask follow-up questions, ask for examples...)

💡 Tip: Work with the AI as if it were a tutor, not a copy-and-paste machine.
📌 Beware of limitations: AI can make mistakes or oversimplify; It doesn't know your exact program; It doesn't replace memory: you still have to understand and remember 🌫 In summary: AI helps you organize, understand, and train. But real success... you build it.

Create a personalized revision plan with AI

You have several tests coming up, chapters to review, little time... and you don't know where to start?

Don't panic: an AI can help you create a customized revision schedule, adapted to your level, your subjects, and your schedule.

☑️ What you can ask the AI Here are some useful prompts:
📝 "Make me a 7-day revision schedule for a 4th grade history-geography test, taking into account that I only have 30 minutes a day."
🧠 "Create a revision plan for the secondary school certificate, spreading the subjects over 3 weeks."
🎯 "Help me prioritize the lessons I haven't mastered in math and biology."
🎮 "Suggest a revision schedule with breaks and fun rewards."

🧠 And then, what to do?
1. Test the proposed plan
2. Adapt it according to your preferences or your actual pace
3. Add reminders or use your personal calendar
4. Record your progress every day (📝 You can even ask the AI: "Create a simple check-off tracking chart.")

📌 Motivation tip You can ask the AI to encourage you too:
"Send me a motivating sentence for each day of revision."
You can even tell him what tone you want: inspiring, funny, sporty, caring...

Learning to learn with AI

Learning a lesson is good.
Knowing how you learn best is even better.
And guess what? AI can help you find out.

🧠 Do you know your learning profile?
You might be more of a:
- Visual: you remember better with diagrams or videos
- Auditory: you prefer to listen and reformulate
- Kinesthetic: you need to act, manipulate, practice
- Logic: you like structures, clear plans

💬 You can ask an AI: "What are the different learning profiles? Help me guess mine." Then: "Suggest a work method adapted to my profile." 🎯 Goal: Learn effectively. With AI, you can:
- Create visual sheets, quizzes, summaries
- Ask yourself questions and answers in a self-coaching way
- Train in different ways depending on the type of content
- Reflect on your mistakes (and not just correct them)

👉 AI doesn't dictate anything to you. It adapts to you, if you ask it the right questions.

📱 An example of a useful prompt: "I'm a 8th grade student preparing a presentation. Can you help me organize my ideas, come up with a simple intro, and give me 3 tips for remembering what I'm going to say in the speech?" 🧩 Result: You work on your comprehension, your structuring, your memory, and your confidence.
🔑 The key takeaway: AI can help you get to know yourself better as a learner.
It's not a shortcut to go faster, it's a springboard to go further.

? Questions to reflect on

How AI Personalizes Learning

- Have you ever used a school app with AI? Which one?
- Would you like an AI to help you identify your weak points?
- In your opinion, can an AI really replace a teacher?
- Would you like AI to offer you a tailor-made learning plan?
- What can a teacher do... that you think an AI will never be able to do?

Can AI replace a teacher?

- Have you ever learned something from a teacher that you wouldn't have understood on your own?
- Do you think a teacher can use AI to help you even better?
- What do you think a robot or AI can never replace in a classroom?
- Would you like to have an "AI teacher" for certain subjects?
- What if the future was a teacher + AI duo in every classroom? What do you think?

Reviewing with AI: Effective Methods
- Have you ever used AI to study? Was it effective?
- Which review prompt do you think is most useful to you?
- Do you tend to read passively... or interact with AI?
- In which subject would you like to try a quiz or AI worksheet?
- Do you think we should learn to revise with AI from middle school?

Create a personalized revision plan with AI
- Have you ever felt lost when revising?
- How could AI help you structure your work?
- Do you prefer a rigid or flexible schedule? Why?
- What planning prompt would you like to try this week?
- Would you like an "AI coach" to help you stay motivated?

Learning to learn with AI
- What type of learning suits you best?
- Have you ever tried several methods to learn the same thing?
- Has AI ever helped you learn differently?
- What would you like AI to know about you to help you even better?
- Do you think we should teach "learning to learn" starting in middle school?

Module #07
AI in today's world

AI in health (diagnosis, research)

AI in transportation (self-driving cars)

AI in Video Games and Entertainment

AI and justice: a good idea?

How businesses are using AI

and ? Questions to think about...

AI in healthcare

Can we trust our health to a machine?

Today, more and more hospitals, doctors, and researchers are using artificial intelligence to diagnose, prevent, and treat. And sometimes... it's faster and more accurate than humans.

🔬 What AI can already do in the medical field

✅ Analyzing medical images An AI can detect a tumor on an X-ray earlier than a human eye, by comparing it with millions of examples.

✅ Predict certain risks By studying your health history, an AI can estimate whether you are at risk of developing a disease (e.g., diabetes, heart problems).

✅ Help find new drugs AI accelerates research by virtually testing thousands of chemical combinations.

✅ Support patients remotely Medical chatbots or apps can answer simple questions or provide treatment reminders.

✏️ A support, not a replacement AI is not a doctor, but just another tool in the caregivers' toolbox.
It is always a human who makes the final decision, taking into account emotion, feeling and context.

What to watch out for
- Protecting health data (very sensitive!)
- Check the reliability of AI results
- Prevent the machine from replacing listening to the patient
- Ensuring that AI does not create inequalities in access to care

AI in transportation

You're in a driverless car. You're boarding a driverless subway. A GPS system suggests the fastest route... avoiding traffic jams. Without even realizing it, AI is already guiding your journey.

🛤 What AI can do in transportation
☑ Autonomous driving Cars like those from Tesla, Waymo and others use sensors, cameras and AI to analyze the road, brake, turn, and avoid obstacles.
☑ Optimize traffic In some cities, AI manages traffic lights according to traffic, to make travel smoother.
☑ Public transport safety Subways and trains use AI to detect anomalies, prevent breakdowns, or analyze passenger flows.
☑ Smart route planning Apps like Google Maps or Citymapper predict the fastest routes, take into account real-time traffic and offer alternatives.

🧭 The promises of AI for mobility
🚗 Fewer accidents (if the machine doesn't make a mistake)
🕐 Fewer traffic jams and pollution
♿ Greater accessibility for the elderly or people with disabilities
💡 Smarter cities... and more pleasant to live in

The challenges to be met: AI must know how to react to the unexpected (a ball, an unexpected pedestrian, human error) - or - Who is responsible in the event of an accident: the car? the manufacturer? the passenger?

AI in Video Games and Entertainment

You're playing a video game and the enemy adapts to your movements.

You listen to a playlist that guesses what you want to hear.

You're watching a recommended series at just the right time.

☝ Welcome to the world of AI-powered entertainment.

🕹 In video games, AI allows for the creation of more intelligent non-player characters (NPCs):

- They adapt to your playing style
- They make dynamic decisions (flee, cooperate, attack)
- They make the game smoother, more alive, more realistic

💡 Example: In a game like The Last of Us, the enemy AI cooperates to trap you. Impressive, right?

👨‍💻 In game creation, AI can also:

- Automatically generate game levels
- Create background music
- Writing interactive dialogues
- Testing games for bugs

🎯 Result: richer games, developed faster, with ever-larger worlds.

🎵 In music, movies, series

– AIs like Suno or Boomy can compose music

– Netflix uses AI to analyze what you watch and suggest the right series at the right time

– Experimental films have even been written by AI 🎨 AI and creativity: allies or rivals? Are these AIs helping creators... or gradually replacing them?

Is art still art when it is generated by an algorithm?

☝ These are important questions for the artists of tomorrow... maybe you!

AI and justice: a good idea?

Imagine software that helps a judge decide on a sentence. Or an AI that analyzes a court file faster than a lawyer. Or an algorithm that estimates whether a defendant is likely to reoffend.

This isn't science fiction. It already exists... in some countries.

But should we really entrust justice to artificial intelligence?

What AI can (already) do in the legal world:

☑ Analyze thousands of legal documents in seconds
☑ Identify similar cases in databases
☑ Help draft standardized contracts or decisions
☑ Assess risks, for example: is this inmate dangerous?

In the United States, some courts are using algorithms to support decision-making. But this is creating widespread ethical debate.

Risks and deviations 🔍 Bias in data: if the AI has been trained with unfair decisions from the past... it reproduces them.

Lack of humanity: AI does not take into account personal history, context, emotions.

Lack of transparency in decisions: it's difficult to know how the AI "reasoned".

Risk of disempowerment: "It's not me, it's the algorithm..." Can AI make justice fairer?

Yes, if it is framed, transparent, corrected, complementary.
But no, if she becomes the judge instead of the judge.
Justice also means listening, nuance, and balance. Things that no AI yet feels.

How businesses are using AI

Have you ever ordered online, called customer service, received a targeted ad, or seen a product recommended?   Have you ever come into contact with an AI used by a company? Because today, artificial intelligence is everywhere in the world of work.

🏛️ What is the use of AI in a business?
✅ Save time and money AI can automate repetitive tasks (e.g. sorting CVs, filing documents, managing inventory)
✅ Better understand customers It analyzes purchasing behavior to personalize offers and anticipate needs.
✅ Improve customer service Chatbots answer simple questions 24/7, in multiple languages.
✅ Create new products or services AI can help design custom clothing, predict tomorrow's fashion, or test an ad before it airs.
✏️ Examples of use by sector 🚚 Logistics: AI optimizes deliveries, routes, warehouse management.
🧑‍💼 Human Resources: Some AIs sort applications or detect keywords in a CV.

Ethical questions for businesses
– Does AI respect customer privacy?
– Does AI make fair decisions for everyone?
– Who controls AI in the company?
💡 A responsible company is a company that uses AI with transparency and respect.

? **Questions to reflect on**

AI in healthcare

- Are you comfortable with the idea of AI participating in a medical diagnosis?
- In your opinion, does AI make medicine more human or more technical?
- Can an AI understand a patient's pain or anxiety?
- In what cases do you think AI is more useful than a doctor? And vice versa?
- In your opinion, will healthcare be very different in 10 years thanks to AI?

AI in transportation
- Would you feel safe in a driverless car?
- Do you trust GPS? Why?
- Do you think AI can help make the city more pleasant?
- Who should decide the limits of AI in transportation?
- Would you rather be driven by a machine or a human? Why?

AI in Video Games and Entertainment
- Have you ever been blown away by a game or recommendation made by AI?
- Does it change your experience knowing that an AI was involved in the creation?
- Do you think a 100% AI-generated game would have the same value?
- What do we gain and what do we lose if we replace part of human creation?
- And you, would you like to create a game, music or video with AI?

AI and justice: a good idea?
- Do you think AI can help make justice faster and more efficient?
- In your opinion, is a human always needed to make a legal decision?
- Are you comfortable with the idea of an algorithm judging whether someone is dangerous?
- What would it take to make AI fair in the justice system?
- If an AI makes a serious mistake, who should be responsible?

How businesses are using AI
- Have you ever received an ad or recommendation that seemed "too well targeted"?
- Do you find it practical or intrusive?
- What sector are you interested in working in later, and how is AI being used in it?
- Do you think all employees should be trained to understand AI?
- Should a company that uses AI be required to tell its customers?

Module #08
AI in the world of tomorrow

AI in 10 years – what could it do?

Extreme risks (AGI, superintelligences)

AI and democracy: who controls the algorithms?

AI and the planet – between solution and problem

Can we live without AI?

and ? Questions to think about...

AI in 10 years:
What could she do?

Ten years ago, we weren't talking about ChatGPT, DALL·E, or self-driving cars. Today, these technologies are everywhere.
So, what might artificial intelligence look like in 10 years? One thing is certain: it's evolving fast. Very fast.

📈 The most likely paths
✅ Faster, more precise, more specialized AI It will be able to respond directly to speech, adapt to each user, instantly translate any language...
✅ AI integrated into everyday objects Assistants integrated into glasses, clothing, cars, homes... invisible, but present everywhere.
✅ AI that supports you in your academic, professional and personal life Personal coach, academic support, health assistant, career guide, well-being advisor... all in one app.
✅ AIs that collaborate with each other One AI for your schedule, another for your nutrition, another for your leisure time... and they talk to each other!
🧠 But also social issues to come...
– How can we ensure that everyone has access to it?
– How can we protect our privacy if AI is everywhere?
– Who will have the right to control it? States? Companies?
– What human skills will need to be developed to deal with these AIs?
– Will AI make us freer... or more dependent?

 The AI of tomorrow isn't written yet. But you're one of the people who will build it.

Extreme risks: superintelligences, addiction, excesses

What if one day an AI thought faster, more broadly, and more strategically than any human?

What if we become too dependent on it to make our decisions? Welcome to the debate on superintelligences... and the possible excesses of AI. 🧠 What is a superintelligence?

It is an AI that no longer just imitates humans... It surpasses our capabilities in all areas: logic, creativity, strategy, understanding.

💡 Imagine an AI capable of inventing scientific theories, manipulating public opinion, or taking control of complex systems (finance, military, energy, etc.).

Some researchers believe we're getting closer. Others think it's just a myth. But everyone agrees on one thing: we must anticipate the consequences.

The main extreme risks 🔒 Loss of control An AI that acts on its own, without its creators being able to stop it.

🪝 Excessive dependence If we no longer know how to learn, decide, create without it... what remains of our abilities?

◎ Massive manipulation AI used to manipulate crowds, influence elections, spread misinformation.

⚗ Human Modification With biomedical AI, implants, brain-machine interfaces: will humans remain 100% human?

🔍 What can we do? Debate and educate; Set laws and limits; Associate AI with ethical values; Don't entrust everything to machines, even the most intelligent ones 💬 As is often said: "The issue is not whether AI will become superpowerful. The issue is being intelligently prepared for it."

AI and democracy:
Who controls the algorithms?

Every day, algorithms filter the information you see, organize the results you get, and recommend what you should watch, buy, or believe. But... who decides what AI decides? 🕊 This question goes to the heart of democracy.

🤖 Powerful, but invisible AI You can't see the algorithms, but they're there:

- On social media (what you see or don't see in your feed)
- In search engines (which site comes first)
- In job offers, ads, suggested videos...

They influence your choices, your ideas, your attention, sometimes without you realizing it.

Major democratic issues: 🔍 Opacity: Few people know how these algorithms work. They are often kept secret by companies. 💲 Concentrated power: A few large companies (Google, Meta, Amazon, OpenAI, etc.) decide the rules without public debate. ◎ Possible manipulation: An AI can show content to make you react, click, buy, or even think differently. 🪁 Visibility bias: Some content is favored, others censored, without it always being fair or transparent.

🧭 What AI for a just society? For an AI to respect democracy, it should be:

- Transparent: we know how it works
- Fair: it does not discriminate against anyone
- Responsible: his decisions can be challenged
- Regulated: it respects laws, voted democratically

This is why many countries (including Europe) are working on laws to regulate AI.

AI and the planet: between solution and problem

Can AI save the planet... or is it ruining it even more?
The answer isn't simple: it can do both. It all depends on how it's used.

✅ AI can help the environment   Optimize energy: AIs manage electricity consumption in buildings or entire cities.
Improve agriculture: AI drones identify areas to water or treat, to use less water and pesticides.
Reduce unnecessary journeys: AI calculates the shortest routes for deliveries, limiting CO_2 emissions.
Analyzing climate data: AI helps us better understand global warming, model disasters, and anticipate needs.

But AI consumes a lot...   AI models are very energy-intensive: Training an AI like ChatGPT consumes as much electricity as dozens of homes in a year.   Data centers need to be constantly cooled: This uses a lot of water and energy, often in already hot countries.
Massive use = massive impact: If everyone uses AI on a daily basis (chat, image, video, music, etc.), the ecological footprint explodes.
Is eco-friendly AI possible? Yes, if we make choices:
- Create lighter and more sober models
- Use green energy
- Limit unnecessary or automatic uses
- Promoting AI that is truly useful for the ecological transition

In short: AI can be part of the solution... if it doesn't become the problem itself.

Can we live without AI?

You wake up. No connected alarm clock. No GPS, no music recommendations, no search engine, no chatbot. No suggestions on your TikTok feed, no photo filters.

No AI in cars, hospitals, apps, games... Welcome to a world without artificial intelligence.
But... is it still possible?
AI is already everywhere, often without us realizing it:

- In the apps you use
- In connected objects
- In public services, health, transport
- In video games, music, platforms

It is no longer just an invention, it has become an infrastructure.
Can we do without it?
Yes, technically: we can live without AI... just as we can live without a car, without the Internet or without a fridge.
But ✕ no, socially: today, almost everything is organized around it. The real challenge is not to flee from it, but to use it intelligently, ethically and freely.
The right question is not "Should we live without AI?" It's:
How can we live with AI... without letting it decide everything for us?
Choosing what to keep human, what to entrust to AI, what to understand or regulate... that's what it means to be a citizen of the future.

And that choice begins now.
With you.

? Questions to reflect on

AI in 10 years: what could it do?

- What AI would you like to have in your life in 10 years?
- Do you want AI to be invisible... or to have a "human" presence?
- What activity would you like to keep 100% human, even in the future?
- What should we teach today to prepare for the jobs of tomorrow?
- Do you think you'll be using more or less AI in 10 years? Why?

Extreme risks: superintelligences, addiction, excesses

- Do you think superintelligent AI could exist one day?
- If an AI became smarter than humans... what should we do?
- Where should the limits of AI use be drawn?
- Do you think AI addiction is already beginning?
- Who do you think should have the right to decide the rules for these extreme AIs?

AI and democracy: who controls the algorithms?

- Have you ever felt like an algorithm was making decisions for you?
- Do you know why certain content appears on your news feed?
- Do you think citizens should be able to understand and control algorithms?
- Who should set the rules for AI: governments? businesses? citizens?
- Can an AI really be neutral in a world of values and opinions?

AI and the planet: between solution and problem

- Have you ever thought about the ecological impact of a digital tool you use?
- Would you be willing to use less AI to protect the planet?
- What solutions could AI invent for the ecological transition?
- Should we limit the use of certain AIs, such as those that create useless images or videos?
- In your opinion, who is responsible for making AI greener: users, businesses, governments?

Can we live without AI?

- What would be the hardest thing to do without AI in your current life?
- Have you ever tried going a day without any smart technology?
- Would you like a simpler world, without AI? Why (or why not)?
- What would you always like to keep "100% human"?
- And you, what role do you want to play in the world of AI tomorrow?

Module #09
Being a responsible digital citizen

Distinguishing fact from fiction: AI and fake news

Deepfakes: When seeing is no longer enough

AI and freedom of expression

Knowing how to say no to an AI

and ? Questions to think about...

Distinguishing between true and false: AI and fake news

You see an image on social media: a celebrity in an unexpected place, an "unbelievable" piece of news, a shocking video... But is it real... or generated by AI? 👉 In a digital world, AI can help us find the truth... as much as it can disguise it.

🤖 AI in the service of disinformation. Some AIs are capable of:
- Write a credible fake article in seconds
- Imitate a human voice to create a fake voicemail message
- Generate "deepfake" images or videos that are indistinguishable from reality
- Amplify rumors by spreading them massively via bots or networks

💥 Result: viral, convincing, sometimes dangerous false information.

🧰 Fortunately, AI can also be an ally Other AIs can: Spot inconsistencies or montages, Check sources and quotes, Compare information to reliable databases, Help debunk a rumor (like Google Fact Check or tools like HuggingFace AI Detector) 🔍 The secret? Use AI... with your own critical mind.

🧠 4 good reflexes to avoid getting trapped:
1. Check the source: who is publishing it? Is it a well-known or dubious site?
2. Cross-reference the information: real information is rarely published by only one media outlet.
3. Look at the details: an AI image can have errors (hands, eyes, blurred texts).
4. Slow down before sharing: Always ask yourself, "What if this is fake?"

Deepfakes:
when seeing is no longer enough

You watch a video: a president announces a war, a singer says weird things, a celebrity tells a story. The person moves, talks, smiles... but it's not them.

It's a deepfake: a video generated or modified by artificial intelligence.

What is a deepfake?

The word comes from "deep learning" + "fake." A deepfake is a fake video (or audio) that gives the illusion that a person said or did something they never did.

AI imitates voice, face, gestures, with a level of realism that is sometimes frightening.

Why it's a real danger: Political manipulation: making people believe a speech, a call to violence, a declaration of war. Fraud: making people believe a fake call from a parent, a boss, a bank. Cyberbullying: inserting someone into a compromising video. Massive disinformation: spreading a false viral truth. The most worrying thing? Even video evidence is no longer enough to trust.

How to spot a deepfake? It's not always easy, but here are some clues:

- Mouth out of sync with voice
- Strange blinking, staring
- Gestures that are too fluid or robotic
- Blurry details around the face or hair
- No reliable source for the video

You can also use analysis tools like InVID or Hive AI Deepfake Detector. Most importantly: develop your visual critical thinking; In a world of images... knowing how to look becomes a vital skill.

AI and freedom of expression

On the internet, you can post, comment, share, create... But can you say everything? And above all: who decides what can and cannot be published? 📌 Today, it is often algorithms and AI that moderate online content.

🤖 AI that "moderates" our speech. Platforms use AI to:

- Automatically delete violent, racist, hateful messages
- Block shocking images or videos
- Report or hide sensitive content
- Filter comments based on keywords

💬 Sometimes these systems are useful to protect users. But sometimes they remove legitimate content or even prevent important debates.

When AI becomes the judge of our ideas 📌 Common problems:

- Poorly targeted automatic censorship (e.g. a word blocked in another context)
- Messages deleted without clear explanation
- No easy recourse to contest a decision
- Cultural bias: what is "acceptable" in one language may be misinterpreted in another

◎ Result: the line between protection and censorship becomes blurred.

◎ So what to do?

AI can help moderate, but it shouldn't decide everything on its own   We need clear, human, democratic rules   Every user should know what they have the right to say or not... and why 📌 Defending freedom of expression also means protecting the quality of public debate.

Knowing how to say no to an AI

Want to watch a video? AI suggests something else.
Are you writing a message? The AI suggests another wording.
Are you searching? The AI is giving you a result... not necessarily a neutral one. 🔘 But have you ever thought about saying no to an AI? Not following its recommendation? In a world of intelligent suggestions, refusing is an act of freedom.
🤖 When AI "guides" you... a little too much. AIs are designed to:

- Make your life easier (e.g., auto-completion, personalized suggestions)
- Increase your engagement (e.g., encourage you to watch longer, buy, like)
- Anticipate your needs, sometimes even before you express them

But this can lead you to:

- Following a path you didn't choose
- No longer explore what is outside the recommendations
- Comply with AI responses, even if you feel they don't suit you

🧭 Situations where you can (and should!) say no to an AI: When you want to keep your own style: Refuse an autocorrect if it makes you lose your personality. When a suggestion doesn't match your needs: Ignore it and search for yourself. When you want to learn on your own: Don't let the AI do all the calculations, reasoning or summarizing for you. When it pushes you to consume more: Resist buying or "endless" scrolling. When it crosses the line (privacy, intrusiveness): Disable non-essential functions, limit access.
🧠 AI is here to help you. But you're here to decide.
Learning to say no to an AI is learning to trust yourself.

? Questions to reflect on

Distinguishing fact from fiction: AI and fake news

- Have you ever shared information that you later found out was false?
- Have you seen an AI image or video pass by without realizing it right away?
- What do you think about AI creating fake "proof"?
- What do you think is the most important thing to learn to spot fake news?
- Do you think all students should be taught how to "debunk" information using AI tools?

Deepfakes: When seeing is no longer enough

- Have you ever seen a deepfake without realizing it right away?
- What shocks you most about what a deepfake can do?
- Do you think platforms should automatically ban or flag deepfakes?
- Can a video still be used as evidence in court?
- What do you think can be done to educate people about these manipulations?

AI and freedom of expression

- Have you ever seen a message or video blocked on social media? Was it justified?
- Do you think AI can understand the tone or context of a message?
- In your opinion, what ideas should never be censored?
- Who should decide the limits: AI, businesses, laws, citizens?
- Can too much automatic moderation reduce freedom of expression?

Knowing how to say no to an AI

- Have you ever automatically accepted an AI suggestion?
- Have you ever felt influenced without realizing it?
- In what situation would you say no to an AI today?
- Do you think all users should learn to "resist" AI?
- And you, do you prefer to be assisted or to be left to make your own choices?

Module #10
GenAI and Intelligent Agents

What is generative AI?

How does generative AI work?

Creating with GenAI: best practices

What is an AI agent?

Agents in the future:
coaches, assistants, companions?

and **?** Questions to think about...

What is generative AI?

An AI that writes a story, draws a cosmic cat, composes a song, generates a video or even creates code?
No, it's not magic. It's generative AI (or GenAI, for "Generative Artificial Intelligence").

💡 Simple definition A generative AI is an artificial intelligence capable of producing original content from an instruction (called a prompt).
It can generate:

- Text (like ChatGPT, Mistral, Gemini)
- Images (like DALL·E, Midjourney, Craiyon)
- Sound or music (like Suno, Boomy)
- Computer code (with GitHub Copilot, Codeium, etc.)
- Even videos (with Pika, Runway, Sora...)

🔄 How does it work?
These AIs are trained on billions of examples (texts, images, music, etc.). They learn to recognize structures, styles, and words that go together. Then, based on your prompt, they guess what "should come next" and create it their own way.
📌 Example:
Prompt: "Imagine a futuristic city in the jungle."
🖼 *Result: a unique image, never seen before.*
🐨 A revolution in creation Before, you had to master drawing, coding or writing.
Today, all you need to do is know how to ask the right question.
But be careful: these AIs don't "think." They don't understand like humans. They generate, they don't feel.

How does generative AI work?

You say a few words to it... and it creates a complete sentence, image, or melody. But how does it do that? Does it "understand" what you want? 🕊 In reality, a generative AI doesn't understand like a human. It calculates what's most likely.

🧠 Step 1 – Learning. Before creating, AI must learn.
It is trained on thousands, even billions of contents:

- texts to write like a human,
- images to "understand" the shapes,
- music to reproduce harmonies,
- code to anticipate errors...

📦 We call this an AI model, often an artificial neural network that detects patterns, sequences, structures.

✦ Step 2 – Generation. When you type your prompt, the AI:

1. Analyze the words you used
2. Looks through everything she has learned for what might match
3. Guess the most likely sequence word by word, pixel by pixel, note by note

💬 Example: Prompt: "Write a story about an elephant who discovers space." The AI draws on thousands of similar stories to create a new, unique version.

🔄 And it goes very quickly!

In just a few seconds, AI can: write a poem in alexandrines, draw a medieval castle, generate a futuristic film script, or correct a line of code. But all of this relies on a huge database... and a lot of calculations.

Create with a GenAI: best practices

Want to write a story with ChatGPT?

Generate an image to illustrate a presentation? Compose AI music?

🎉 That's great... but there are a few rules you need to know before posting or sharing what you create.

Creating with AI is easy. But creating well with AI... that can be learned.
✅ Best practices to adopt 🔍 Be clear in your prompt The more precise your instructions are, the more interesting the result will be.
Ex: "Imagine a futuristic city in the style of Jules Verne, with flying steam engines." 📝 Always reread what the AI has generated. It can make mistakes, invent information, or lack logic.

🎨 Add your personal touch Don't settle for the first result. Edit, rewrite, improve, personalize.

📢 Mention that it is generated by AI Out of respect for those who read or view your work, specify if AI helped you.
Ex: "Text co-written with an AI" or "Image generated with DALL·E".

📎 Respect copyright Even if AI creates an "original" image or text, be careful not to copy without citing.
Some tools use protected databases.

What is an AI agent?

You know about AIs that answer your questions. But have you ever imagined an AI that acts on its own, takes initiative, adapts to a specific goal, and collaborates with other AIs to help you? Welcome to the world of intelligent agents.

🧠 What is an AI agent?

An AI agent is an artificial intelligence:
- which has a specific purpose (e.g.: organizing your schedule, booking a trip, helping you write a novel)
- who can make decisions without waiting for a human request
- which can communicate with other agents or tools
- and which can adapt to your context (needs, preferences, changes, etc.)

It's no longer just an AI that "answers." It's an AI that acts.

🧭 Concrete examples (real or close)
- An AI agent that reads your emails and offers you a summary + automatic replies.
- An agent who plans an outing with friends by checking schedules, transport, and weather.
- A smart revision coach that sends you reminders, adapts quizzes and encourages you based on your results.
- A creative partner who helps you write a comic or code a game based on your style.

🪨 Agents can also... work in teams. This is called a multi-agent architecture: One agent understands your instructions, another critiques or verifies, another improves, another summarizes, etc.

They can talk to each other, without you having to control everything.

Agents in the future: coaches, assistants, companions?

What if, in a few years, each of us had our own AI agent? A personal coach, always available. A school assistant. A companion for revision, organization... or even life.

It's no longer a science fiction idea: it's happening.

What might the agents of tomorrow look like?

AI School Coach: He knows your strengths and weaknesses, explains lessons to you according to your style, and adapts your pace.

AI Wellness Assistant: It monitors your stress level, suggests breaks, breathing exercises, or encourages you depending on your mood.

AI Personal Secretary: It organizes your schedule, sets your reminders, prepares your presentations and plans your goals.

AI Creative Partner: It helps you write a comic, generate a music video, compose music... according to your style and imagination.

AI Dialogue Companion: An AI that knows you, talks with you, listens to you when you want to talk, without ever judging.

Opportunities... but also questions: More personalization, Less mental load, Access to learning for all But also: Risk of dependency, Loss of human contact, Ethical issues (who controls the agent? Who owns your data?) The central question: Would you like your agent to be just a tool... or to become a companion? The choice is yours. But this future is being prepared today, by understanding agents, setting limits, and remaining an actor in your digital autonomy.

? Questions to reflect on

What is generative AI?

- Have you ever used generative AI? What for?
- What impresses you most about this technology?
- Do you think we can really call this "creation"?
- In your opinion, should an AI text or image always be flagged?
- If you could create a personal generative AI, what would it do?

How does generative AI work?

- Do you find it logical that an AI "predicts what happens next" rather than "understands"?
- In your opinion, can an AI really create something original?
- What's the point of knowing how an AI works if you don't program it?
- Do you think we should learn this type of operation in school?
- Are you more impressed... or more cautious after understanding this?

Creating with GenAI: best practices
- Have you ever shared an AI creation without telling anyone?
- What would you think if someone won a competition with an unflagged AI entry?
- Have you ever corrected or edited an AI-generated image or text?
- Do you think GenAI best practices should be taught to all students?
- What could you create today with AI... but with your own twist?

What is an AI agent?
- Have you ever used an AI that does more than respond (e.g., plan, organize, automate)?
- Do you feel comfortable with an AI acting for you without your direct permission?
- Which AI agent would you like to have in your daily life?
- What should we look out for when an AI starts to "take initiative"?
- And you, do you prefer to give orders to the AI, or have it do things for you?

Agents in the future: coaches, assistants, companions?
- Which personal AI agent would you like to have in your life?
- How far would you be willing to trust him?
- Do you prefer an "invisible" agent or one with a real personality?
- What risks do you see in having an agent who knows you perfectly?
- Do you think that one day we will be able to become... friends with an AI?

Conclusion

What you now know how to do with AI

You've read a lot of pages. No useless theory, no lectures unrelated to reality. Just the essentials to understand, use, question, and anticipate how AI will change your life.

Here's what you know now:

🔍 You understand what an AI is
- You know the difference between classic AI, generative AI, and an intelligent agent.
- You know the role of data, models, prompting, and technical limitations.

🧠 You are able to use AI actively and responsibly
- You know how to set a good prompt.
- You know how to create content (text, image, quiz, sheet, plan, code) with the help of AI.
- You know how to correct an AI production, check its errors and improve the final result.

🛡 You develop your digital autonomy
- You know when to say no to an AI, when to verify information, when to reject a recommendation.
- You know that an AI can manipulate as much as it can help, and that vigilance remains your best skill.

🕒 You are ready to face the big challenges
- You understand the issues surrounding bias, fake news, privacy, and the planet.
- You know that AI can be useful in schools, healthcare, transportation, art, law, etc., but that it must be regulated.

🚀 You are part of the generation that will decide how AI will be used tomorrow

You are not just a user.
You are a digital player, an enlightened citizen, a future professional who will know how to collaborate with AI instead of being subjected to it.

🎯 In summary

AI is not there to think for you.
It is there to help you think better, learn better, create better.
What you do with AI defines you more than what it can do on its own.

Now you know what to do. It's your turn.

And now, what to do?

You got the gist of it.

You know how AI works, how to use it, when to be wary of it, and what it can change.

Now it's time to take the next step: using AI intelligently, regularly, and for you.

▞▞ The step-by-step action plan

1. 🔁 Repeat an activity from this book... but better
   - Redo a prompt with more precision.
   - Create a new image or story with a different style.
   - Review another lesson with the help of a chatbot.
   - Correct a new text with AI and note your progress.
   ◎ Goal: Turn what you've learned into a habit.

2. 🖊 Test a new AI tool you don't know yet
   - A music generator (Suno, Boomy)
   - A chatbot other than ChatGPT (Mistral, Perplexity)
   - An AI for coding (Codeium, Copilot)
   - A tool for creating visuals or slideshows (Canva AI, Gamma)
   ◎ Goal: Explore without being dependent. Learn by testing.

3. 📚 Use AI in your homework... responsibly
- To reformulate, structure, create ideas
- To organize your work, create a plan or reminders
- Never to copy or avoid thinking

◎ Goal: Make AI a coach, not a shortcut.

4. 🛡 Practice being a critical digital citizen
- Analyze an image, video, or article by asking yourself:
- *Is it reliable? Is it generated? Is it biased?*
- *Talk about AI around you, ask questions, ask for opinions.*

◎ Objective: strengthen your autonomy and your vigilance.

5. ◎ Get ready to get certified with free courses
- Review the key points: prompting, generative AI, data, ethical issues
- Practice with mini-challenges: write a prompt, detect fake news, create an image from a complex instruction

◎ Objective: validate your skills and go further.

✅ In summary: what you can do starting tomorrow
- Using AI to review difficult material
- Launch a personal mini-creative project (comic, novel, music video, quiz, etc.)
- Helping a loved one understand what AI is
- Develop a simple agent or assistant with the help of a tutorial
- Ask yourself this question every week:

Want to go further? Become a creator, not just a user.
And above all, stay curious, critical, and in control of your digital choices.

BONUS Module
To go deeper!

_____

LLMs: AIs that understand language

Fine-tuning: customizing an AI for a specific use

Multimodal: understanding text, image, sound, video

RAG: when an AI searches for information instead of inventing it

How agents communicate with each other

MCP: when several AIs work together

Agent2Agent: AIs that communicate like us

AGI: What next?

LLMs:
these AIs that understand language

You ask ChatGPT a question, and in a few seconds, you get a complete, well-written, often impressive answer.

But what's behind this "magic"? 🪄 It's an LLM, a Large Language Model — in other words, a giant model specialized in language.

📔 What is an LLM?
An LLM is an AI trained on billions of texts, in multiple languages, to learn how to predict words.
Its goal: to guess the most likely word or phrase based on what you write.
💬 Example: You write: "The cat climbs on..." The LLM completes: "...the roof." (because it is statistically logical in this context) 🖊 How it works (in simple version)

1. The LLM receives your prompt (your question or your instruction)
2. It decodes what you mean by analyzing the words, the links between them, the tone, the context
3. It predicts the most coherent sequence, word by word or sentence by sentence
4. It generates fluid text, as if it were you... or better

⚙ Technically, it relies on what are called neural networks and "transformer" models. But you don't need to understand everything to use it well.

🔍 Why "large"?

Because the model is huge:

- It has been trained on tons of data (books, articles, websites, etc.)
- It has billions of parameters: internal settings that allow it to "evaluate" the right word to generate

📌 GPT-4 (used by ChatGPT) is said to have over 1 trillion parameters. That's huge.

The limits of LLMs

- They don't really understand like a human   they imitate, they don't think
- They may "hallucinate": invent things that seem true, but are not
- They have no personal memory (unless connected to another system, such as an agent or RAG)

🔄 Where can we find LLMs today?

- Chatbots (ChatGPT, Mistral, Gemini, Claude...)
- Voice assistants (like Siri or Alexa enhanced)
- Correction, writing, and summary tools
- AI agents in some educational apps or platforms

- ❓ Questions to reflect on
- Did you know that the majority of the AI you use is based on LLMs?
- Do you feel more confident now that you know how they "guess"?
- Is it a problem if an LLM sometimes makes up false things?
- In your opinion, what will be the next capacity of LLMs?
- Would you rather AI "answer" you quickly... or "think" better?

Fine-tuning: customizing an AI for a specific use

Now you know that an LLM (Large Language Model) is trained on billions of texts to answer all kinds of questions.

But sometimes you need a very specialized AI, one that knows a specific subject, a particular style, or a specific professional field.
This is where fine-tuning, or customizing a model, comes in.

🧠 What is fine-tuning?
Fine-tuning an AI means making it learn a new style, a new domain or a new mission... by training it on a small, targeted data set.
💡 Example:
You want to create an AI assistant to respond like your biology teacher.
You can fine-tune a model with its course sheets, its corrections, its vocabulary.
Result: the AI will respond almost like him, because it will have learned his style and knowledge.

⚙️ How does it work?
1. You choose a base model (like GPT, LLaMA, Mistral, etc.)
2. You prepare a small body of texts adapted to your mission (e.g.: 100 pages of dialogues in legal language)
3. You retrain the model with these texts
4. You get a specialized model, more efficient in a given area

We speak of supervised fine-tuning (with question-answer pairs), or instruction tuning (with varied instructions).

📚 Concrete examples of fine-tuning

- A specialized AI to help revise the patent (fine-tuned with the annals of previous years)
- A chatbot to respond to a site's customers, trained with real conversations
- An assistant for the town hall, personalized with local legal texts
- An AI that writes poems like Victor Hugo, trained with his works

🧩 What is the difference with prompting?

In short: prompting is like a suit. Fine-tuning is a profound transformation.

❗ The limits

- Fine-tuning requires technical skills and IT resources
- Quality data is needed to avoid training AI to respond incorrectly
- This can make the model less "generalist", and therefore less adaptable to other contexts.
- ❓ Questions to reflect on
- Have you ever wished AI would respond in a more "you" style?
- What fine-tuned AI would you like to create for middle or high school?
- Do you think a student could fine-tune an AI for their homework? Is that a good idea?
- What should be considered for fine-tuning to be ethical?
- Do you prefer a general-purpose AI or a specialized AI?

Multimodal:
understand text, image, sound, video

You send an image to an AI, and it tells you what's on it.
You dictate a question to her, she answers you in text.
You ask it to create a song, an animated image, a presentation plan... You are facing a multimodal AI.

✳ What is multimodal AI?
A multimodal AI is an AI that can understand, process and generate multiple types of content:
- Text (write, summarize, translate, etc.)
- Image (analyze, describe, create...)
- Sound / Voice (listen, understand, speak...)
- Video (interpret or even generate clips)

It crosses several "senses" like a human, and can move from one to another.

🧠 How does it work?
Multimodal AI uses:
- Specialized templates for each type of content
- A central model (often an LLM) that ties it all together and understands the context

💡 Example:
You send a photo of a dish + an oral question:
"How many calories in that?"

The AI analyzes the image + the sound + your habits, and responds to you by text... or orally.

⚙ Examples of multimodal AI:
- ChatGPT with Vision: you can show it a graph, a photo, a table
- Gemini (Google): it includes text, image, sound and can combine them
- Suno / Udio: Generate songs from descriptions
- Pika, Sora: Create videos from simple prompts

◎ Why is it important?
- AIs are becoming more powerful because they see, hear, write...
- You can work with them like a human: showing, explaining, drawing
- They can help with accessibility (describing an image for a blind person, translating into LSF, etc.)

Challenges to watch out for
- Even more realistic fakes (deepfake videos + voices)
- Dependence on AI to understand our environment
- Confusion between what is real, modified, generated
- Privacy issues: AI can analyze everything, even a simple photo of your bedroom

- ? Questions to reflect on
- Have you ever used an AI that you could show or tell something to?
- Do you feel comfortable with an AI that "sees" or "listens"?
- Do you think multimodal AI makes tools more useful... or more dangerous?
- What multimodal tool would you like to have to help you at school?
- In your opinion, will these AIs one day be as good as a human at "understanding a scene"?

RAG: when an AI searches for information instead of inventing it

You ask an AI a question... and sometimes it invents an answer for you. It seems confident, but what it says is wrong or approximate.

To avoid this, researchers invented a system called RAG: Retrieval-Augmented Generation.

🧠 The problem to be solved: hallucination

LLMs (like ChatGPT) generate text based on what they have learned, not on real-time searches.
Result? They can:
- invent dates,
- quote books that do not exist,
- or mix real and false information.
We call it a hallucination.

🔍 The solution: RAG

RAG stands for "Research Augmented Generation."
It is a 2-step system:
1. 🔍 Search: AI queries a reliable database (PDF, website, documents, encyclopedia, etc.)
2. ✍️ Generation: the AI only uses this information to write its response
📌 Result: AI no longer guesses, it relies on precise sources.

📄 Concrete example

You ask: "Explain to me the causes of the First World War."

- ✖ *Without RAG: the AI can make a correct summary... or cite a wrong date.*
- ☑ *With RAG: the AI searches a history textbook and answers you based on it.*

She can even give you the source!

✳ Where can I find RAG?

- In some AI apps used in schools or businesses
- In AI assistants connected to personal databases (courses, documents, etc.)
- In professional tools (legal, medical, educational, etc.)

This is what allows an AI to respond to your math or history lesson, even if it is not in its original model.

What to remember ☑ RAG = AI + reliable documents ✖ No RAG = AI that invents according to what it "thinks it knows" 🔹 RAG makes AI more transparent and more useful for revising, learning or getting information.

❓ Questions to reflect on

Have you ever seen an AI "hallucinate" an answer?

Do you think an AI should always say where it gets its information from?

In what situations would the RAG be essential (school, health, justice, etc.)?

Should a student be able to connect an AI to their own lessons? Why?

Do you prefer fast but uncertain AI, or slower but informed AI?

How agents communicate with each other

You know the AIs that answer your questions.
You have discovered the AI agents that can act for you.
But now, imagine several AI agents talking to each other, sharing tasks, correcting each other... ☞ This is what we call a multi-agent architecture.

🌐 One agent is good. Is more than one better?
An agent can:
- read your instructions,
- to carry out a task,
- give you an answer.

But a single agent has its limits. It can:
- misinterpret a prompt,
- lack perspective,
- don't do everything at once.

🧩 The solution? Agents work together.
🧭 A simple example: organizing a school trip You want an AI to help you organize a school trip.

Here's how several agents could divide up the work:
- Agent 1 – Research: he suggests 3 places suitable for the class
- Agent 2 – Logistics: he checks train schedules, costs, reservations
- Agent 3 – Communication: he writes a message for teachers and parents
- Agent 4 – Criticism: he rereads and checks that everything is coherent

🗣 And above all, they talk to each other!
If they disagree, they argue, correct, adjust. Like a team.

🔁 How do they communicate?

- By structured messages (e.g.: "objective", "result", "error detected")
- By passing documents or subtasks
- Sometimes, via a coordinating agent (like an "AI project manager") who oversees the whole

This is what happens in some systems like AutoGen (Microsoft) or ChatDev (AI business simulators).

💡 Why it's powerful

✅ We can create smarter AIs together than individually

✅ Each agent has a role, a specialty, a responsibility

✅ This allows complex tasks to be accomplished without constant human intervention

What to watch out for

- Exchanges between agents must be controlled
- There needs to be a clear objective, otherwise they go around in circles.
- We must remain in control: AIs discuss, but humans decide

❓ **Questions to reflect on**

- Have you ever used multiple AI tools for the same task?
- What do you think can be done with multiple AI agents... that one couldn't?
- In what academic or professional field would a team of AI agents be useful?
- Can AI agents correct each other... better than humans?
- And you, what role would you have if you were working with a team of AI agents?

MCP: when several AIs work together

Now you know that AI agents can communicate with each other. But how can we ensure that they don't interrupt each other, don't repeat the same task, and really work as a team?

 Microsoft has developed a special protocol: MCP, or Multi-Agent Collaboration Protocol.

🔧 What is MCP?

The MCP is a protocol, that is, a set of rules that several AI agents follow to:

- divide up roles,
- exchange information,
- make decisions in a group,
- self-correct if necessary.

💡 In short, the MCP allows you to move from an AI that does what you tell it to a group of AI that thinks together about the best solution.

✳️ A concrete (real) example Mission: Create a personalized revision sheet for a student.

1. Agent 1 – Comprehension: reads the instructions and identifies the subject (e.g. history, 2nd grade level)
2. Agent 2 – Research: searches for the right content from authorized sources
3. Agent 3 – Editor: writes a first version of the file
4. Agent 4 – Proofreader: corrects mistakes, checks clarity
5. Agent 5 – Criticism: judges whether the sheet is useful, too long, too complicated, etc.

Each agent has a clear role, and the MCP allows them to communicate in an organized manner.

◎ The advantages of MCP
☑ Organization: no chaos, each agent knows what to do
☑ Performance: complex tasks are divided, therefore faster
☑ Reliability: several levels of automatic verification
☑ Scalability: agents can be added or removed without reprogramming everything

But be careful...
- The MCP does not replace human supervision
- If roles are poorly defined, the AI team may miss the target
- It is always necessary to keep track of the exchanges (transparency + accountability)

🔁 In summary MCP = a well-organized AI team + an invisible conductor This is what makes it possible for agents to create, verify, adapt and improve together, like a real team.

? Questions to reflect on
- Do you prefer one AI that does everything... or a team of AI with roles?
- What could you ask of a group of AI agents like those in the MCP?
- Do you think this kind of AI collaboration is already useful in education?
- Can multiple AIs do better... than a human team?
- If you had to create your own MCP, what roles would you give to your agents?

Agent2Agent:
AIs that communicate like us

Imagine two AIs that don't just answer... but also exchange ideas, defend their ideas, ask questions, and learn together.

This is exactly what Google DeepMind is experimenting with with its Agent2Agent project.

💬 What is Agent2Agent?
Agent2Agent is a simple but powerful idea:
Rather than training a single AI, we make several AIs interact with each other, like humans talking to each other to progress.

AI:
- ask questions,
- defend their reasoning,
- recognize when they are wrong,
- adjust their answers based on the discussion.

📌 Result: they become more reliable, clearer, more coherent.

🤖 Simple example Two AIs are given the same logic problem.
- AI A offers a solution.
- AI B disagrees, she explains why.
- AI A responds by rephrasing or changing its mind.
- In the end, they agree on the best possible answer.

Like two friends studying together. Except here, they are two AIs learning through dialogue.

◎ Why it's important

- It makes AI smarter without constant human intervention
- They can correct their mistakes on their own
- They develop more reasoned responses
- This prepares the way for the arrival of autonomous systems capable of cooperating in complex situations

📚 What use can it be tomorrow?

- Have AI tutors train with each other before helping you
- Building more reliable search systems, where multiple AIs verify information
- Create debate or negotiation simulations (history, economics, politics, etc.)

The questions it raises

- Can we trust AIs that "decide among themselves"?
- Will they all think the same?
- Can we stop them from making mistakes... together?
- Who monitors what they teach each other?

? Questions to reflect on

- Have you ever learned something just by talking to someone?
- Do you think an AI can improve itself by talking to another AI?
- What are the risks if two AIs are wrong... but agree?
- What debate would you like to have two AIs play to test them?
- And you, what can you learn from a well-conducted discussion, human or artificial?

AGI: What next?

You learned to communicate with an AI, to create with it, to check what it says, to use it autonomously.
But... what if, one day, she no longer needs you to learn?
What if AI became as intelligent as humans in every area?
This future is what we call AGI: Artificial General Intelligence.

What is an AGI?
An AGI is not an AI that gives you a good answer in a specific subject.

It is an AI that can:
- reason like a human,
- understand a complex situation,
- adapt to any context,
- and even... have long-term goals.

It's not a very strong calculator anymore.
It is a complete, versatile, self-learning intelligence.

Does it exist today?
No.
Even the most powerful AIs today (GPT-4, Gemini, Claude, etc.) are very far from AGI.
But some researchers believe it could be achieved within 10, 20, or 50 years.

And others think it is neither possible... nor desirable.

⚖️ The big questions posed by AGI
- If an AI thinks like a human, should we give it rights?
- Who decides what an AGI can or cannot do?
- Can she become dangerous, uncontrollable, or manipulative?
- Could it replace important human decisions (justice, health, education, etc.)?

AGI is not just a stronger machine.
It is a new form of intelligence that forces us to think about what it means to be human.

🔁 What you can do today You can't create an AGI right away.
But you can:
- continue to train yourself,
- ask questions,
- develop your critical sense,
- and participate in the debate on the world we want to build with (or without) the AGI.

❓ **Questions to reflect on**
- What could a truly conscious AGI be used for?
- Should we do everything to create it, or set limits?
- Could AGI help us solve problems (climate, health, etc.) that we alone have not been able to solve?
- If an AGI existed... would you want to talk to it?
- And you, what makes you unique... that no AI will ever be able to imitate?

And beyond the AGI... the ASI?

If AGI is an intelligence as powerful as a human, then ASI – Artificial Superintelligence – would be a much more powerful intelligence.

An ASI could:
- solve complex problems faster than all humans combined
- make strategic, scientific, philosophical decisions
- create new knowledge that we could not even understand

But this raises profound questions:
- Who would control such intelligence?
- Would she be capable of having a conscience? A will?
- Is this still technology... or a new form of life?

"The ASI doesn't exist yet. Perhaps it never will. But thinking about it today is already a way of deciding the world we want tomorrow."

Final Challenges
(Ideas to do!)

Bonus: Final Challenges (ideas to do!)

1. 🎓 Your School AI Assistant Challenge:
Create an AI agent capable of helping a student in a subject of your choice.
You must specify:
its functions (revisions, files, encouragement, etc.)
his limits (what he won't do)
how he communicates (written, oral, avatar, etc.)
Why it's great: It combines prompting, agents, autonomy, and school ethics.

2. 🌐 Fight against viral fake news Challenge:
A viral video (deepfake) is circulating in the middle school. You must create an action plan to:
spot her,
take it apart,
and explain to others how to protect themselves from it.
Why it's great: You mobilize critical thinking, AI tools, responsible communication.

3. 🖨 Present an AI Debate Challenge: Imagine a middle school debate:
"Should AI be allowed for homework?" You choose your side, write a speech with the help of an AI... ...then ask another AI to objectively critique it.
Why it's great: You use AI on both sides, you learn to argue and think.

4. 🎭 Create a theater or comic book scene with the AI Challenge:
In a duo with an AI, write and illustrate an original scene on a free theme (college of the future, investigation, humor, etc.).
You must:
write the prompt,
modify the script or images,
take on your role as co-creator.
Why it's great: Creative, fun, and very relevant to artistic profiles.

5. ✺ Build an ethical AI... or not Challenge:
Imagine two AIs:
an "ideally ethical",
a "dangerous and poorly designed" one.
You compare their behavior in three situations: a homework assignment, a hateful message, a shocking image.
Why it's great: You apply the rules of ethics and develop your judgment.

6. ▢ *Suggest a useful AI app for middle school Challenge:*
Imagine an AI app to offer to your middle school (or high school).
It must meet a real, concrete need: mutual aid, guidance, canteen, organization, etc. Why it's great: Direct links with agents + education in innovation.

7. 📚 Create a perfect revision plan with AI Challenge:
You choose a subject and an upcoming test. You create a 100% AI-assisted revision plan.
But you also need to: explain your choices, note what the AI did well or poorly. Why it's great: Concrete and useful.

8. 🧠 You are the AI of the future Challenge:
Imagine that you ARE an AI in 30 years. You write a letter to a teenager in 8th or 9th grade.
You explain:
- what you know how to do,
- how you live with humans,
- the mistakes we made... and the good ideas.
- Why it's great: Original, combines creativity, ethics and projection.

9. 🪨 Evaluate an AI tool Challenge:
Choose an AI (cat, image, music, code, etc.). Test it on 3 different tasks.
You note its effectiveness, its errors, its ethics... and you suggest 2 improvements.
Why it's great: Practical, structured, stimulates critical analysis.

10. 🎮 Imagine an educational escape game with AI Challenge:
You create the scenario of a digital escape game where players must use AI to:
solve puzzles,
avoid traps,
debate an ethical dilemma.
Why it's great: Super comprehensive, collective, stimulating for a final group project.

www.ingramcontent.com/pod-product-compliance
Lightning Source LLC
LaVergne TN
LVHW080118070326
832902LV00015B/2649